A Home for Mom and Dad

Navigating the Nursing Home Maze

Donna Fry, RN, BSN

ISBN: 978-0-692-22597-4

Contents

Foreword

My mother died 3 days short of her 99th birthday. She often said she would not change a thing in her life – she was content and felt blessed with a long lifetime of love and family.

For most of those years, Mom lived independently or with some assistance. But not so for the last 2 years of her life. As her daughter, I recognized that she needed more support in a safe place but felt overwhelmed on where to start to "figure it out."

The decision to move a beloved mother to a nursing home was just the beginning – so many questions to consider .... So many emotions to deal with. Since I had no experience I could draw upon to help me navigate the maze, I stumbled through the process.

A Home for Mom and Dad is a map to help you navigate the maze if you find yourself in this situation. Donna writes not only from her hands-on experience (the best kind) but from her heart. Each chapter builds on the previous one to fill in the navigation map.

With help from Donna's publication, the task becomes less daunting and certainly more manageable. Ultimately everyone benefits from a decision well thought out – the elderly loved one and each family member.

Jean Carleton

Preface

This book was written for families like mine. Many years ago my grandmother became ill and was taken to a local hospital. The hospital social worker had not spoken to my mother about Nanny's discharge, therefore it was a shock to our family to learn that she was going to a local nursing home – neither she nor the family was consulted.

As a Registered Nurse, BSN, with over twenty years of experience working in nursing homes in Eastern Pennsylvania, I have given medication and treatments, and have worked with doctors regarding resident needs. I have held the position of supervisor, monitoring staff who work the floors as I did, giving tours to families needing to place relatives in a safe environment, and addressing problems with family members, staff and administration. I have worked in homes which cater to the wealthy and those filled with residents dependent on Medicaid.

Choosing a nursing home for yourself or someone you love can be a challenging and difficult situation. Families and residents alike have to adjust to a new way of life, often one that was not planned. Maybe a member of the family went to the hospital and although not admitted, was not able to return to their home alone for safety reasons. Or, as often happens, a family member becomes incontinent and is no longer considered manageable by the family. Families are often overwhelmed by the decisions they must make for themselves and their loved ones, and emotions can run high during this process.

When the time to enter a nursing home comes, it is never easy and problems are often not anticipated. It is my intention to help negotiate some of the difficulties that can come up all too frequently for families who find themselves having to make difficult decisions with little information. I hope to help you through this process by giving information you can use to learn about nursing homes and life in them for the residents and their families.

~ Donna Fry

Acknowledgments

Today as I look back on writing this book I feel such gratitude for the loving encouragement I received from my friend and mentor John Davis. John's encouragement, suggestions and unfailing support have made this a wonderful journey.

I am also thankful for the love, direction and strength of Holly Matson. Holly's editing has brought out the inner essence of this book while she has kept me on track and moving forward.

A special thanks to my mother, Jane Moreland, who has spent countless hours discussing, reading and making suggestions to make this an easy read while giving information which I believe is needed by those who are faced with difficult decisions regarding their loved ones. And to my husband who has patiently waited while I worked on this special project.

I am also grateful for all the wonderful families and fellow staff members who have provided the foundation of this book.

~ D.F.

Introduction

It is sad to think that in 1997 there were over 16,000 nursing homes needed in the United States alone. The day when we could keep our parents at home and care for them as they cared for us when we were young seems to be gone.

Nationwide, all nursing homes must be in compliance with Title VI, which requires nursing homes to admit and treat residents without regard to age, sex, ancestry, race, color, national origin, religious creed, or disability. There is to be no distinction in eligibility, or in the manner of providing any resident service by or through the home, based on these criteria.

However, acceptance of residents may be based on availability of rooms and methods of payment. Those with insurance that covers nursing home placement or other sources of funding are usually accepted more easily.

It can be very difficult to place a family member who is dependent on Medicaid. Because our government pays very little for the care of those who are funded by Medicaid, many nursing homes limit the number of beds available to those applicants. Statistics show that many homes with more than 50%

Medicaid beds often close for lack of funds to run the facility, therefore limiting the number of those beds available is a very common practice.

In 1997, adults 65 and older made up 13% of our total population. There are a staggering number of elderly among us and their care must be a prime concern. The financial aspect of living in a nursing home, with 8% of the residents funded by Medicare, 68% funded by Medicaid and only 23% private pay leads one to question: How do facilities fund their services? In understanding these statistics, we can have some awareness of the limited funds available for the care of our elderly.

Chapter 1: Making the Decision

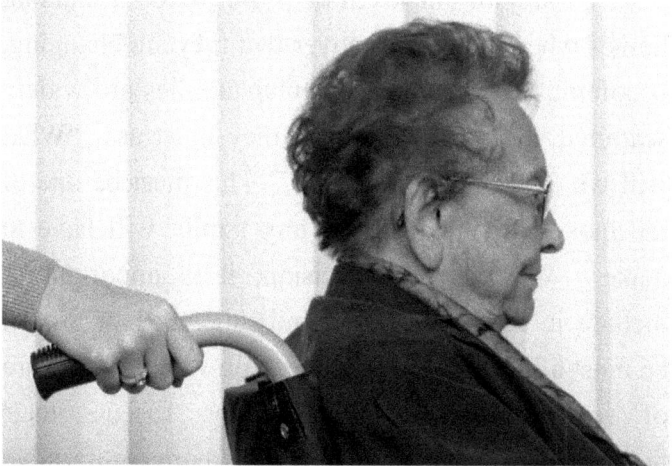

There are many reasons to consider placement in a nursing home. In my experience it is not the first choice of families to place their loved ones in the care of even a well-managed home. Our lifestyles have changed over the years and it takes the concerted effort of many family members to manage the frail and sick among them for long periods of time. In today's society many family members find they must work, which often leaves times when no one is available to care for frail and elderly family members. This is stressful for everyone, not only for those who make the final decision, but also for those who disagree with the decision or were not involved in the process.

Many of our loved ones are placed in nursing homes when families discover that they are changing, becoming less independent. Our families are widely scattered and come to realize they must ask, "What will we do with Mom or Dad?" This must be one of the most difficult decisions any family will have to make. Whatever the decision, it is important to include in discussions all family members who will be most affected by the change. You want to be aware of your loved one's expectations; discuss their feelings and what might make them more comfortable in a new living situation. It is important to begin this process early.

Because of the complexity of the situation, families often have to work through emotions long after placement of an elderly loved one. Be aware that it may be best to seek help in working through family issues. Guilt, anger, distrust, a sense of betrayal and failure can complicate family dynamics. It is never an easy decision and some family members may question the choices made.

This may be a good time to discuss a living will and a Health Care Power of Attorney. Check with your attorney and financial advisor about other necessary documents. Ask the loved one, "What do you want done in the event something should happen that would prevent you from making health care decisions?"

My own mother and I have discussions about if and when a time may come in which I have to make decisions for her. These discussions are open ended, and I withhold my judgments and respect her choices. By doing this I know that the decisions I make on her behalf will be based on what she wants and not on my emotions at the moment of crisis.

Reasons for Admission to a Nursing Home

Residents in nursing homes often live longer than those living at home. The staff in a nursing home is trained to recognize health problems such as urinary tract infections or sepsis much faster than a non-medical caregiver. These conditions can be extremely serious and could require a trip to the emergency room and possible admission for treatment if not recognized early in the course of the illness.

I have often given nursing home tours to families when they are rushed and pressured by our health care system to place their loved ones in a safe environment. If our elderly are judged to be unable to care for themselves, or conditions have come to a point in which the family is no longer able to give adequate care, placement in a nursing home is often recommended by health care providers.

It is also becoming more common for nursing homes to receive residents who have fallen, become ill or confused and were taken to the hospital's emergency room. The patient may not be a candidate to be admitted to the hospital, but when assessed it may have been found that their home situation is unsafe without medical supervision or home care. These patients will be admitted to a nursing home directly from the emergency room. When this happens families come into the nursing home for a tour in a fast paced search for placement. As in the case with my grandmother, hospitals sometimes transfer patients to nursing homes without the knowledge of their family members. When this happens families are not given the opportunity to choose the home they feel is best for their loved one. These families are often angry and confused by the whole process.

Types of Residence Care

Respite Care

There are sometimes "short term" stays in nursing homes, called respite stays. Respite is a service nursing homes offer to families who may need a safe place for their loved ones while they vacation, are ill themselves or have experienced a problem with the environment in which they live. I have had new residents who stayed in the home where I work while the electric service was being restored after a storm or other repairs were being done to their homes. These stays can be as short as overnight to several weeks, depending on the circumstances for the caregivers. Respite care can often serve as a test visit for potential future admission to the home.

The nursing home where I currently work has residents who were volunteers or staff members, and even the postman who delivered mail to the facility. Some have been with us previously for short term stays or respite, and came back to live when the time came and they could no longer manage at home. When this happens, staff welcomes them and they are generally happy to see that people they know are going to be caring for them once again. I think that it is easier for someone coming in for respite who knows they are going home again, and that they can later choose a home they are familiar with. Entering a nursing home is always difficult, but knowing the staff can be a very real comfort.

Rehabilitation

If you are looking for a rehabilitation center, what does the equipment look like? What is the educational requirement to work in the department? What course of rehabilitation can be expected for someone with your loved one's history? Are residents dropped from rehabilitation? Ask why this could happen? Can you come to sessions with your loved one? Can you meet a therapist? Are they open and willing to answer your questions?

Ask if the facility has a rehab floor or if the rehab patients are mixed in with the general population. Patients have the right to refuse rehabilitation. What is the policy if the patient refuses? Make your wishes clear regarding possible refusal of service. If your loved one refuses, do you want a family member to be called to encourage participation in the program that was set up? Make it clear that you want the best for your loved one. Be aware that residents in for rehabilitation sometimes convert to long term residents because they refuse therapy and do not progress to the point at which they are able to return to the community.

Rehabilitation is provided in three areas of care: physical therapy, occupational therapy and speech therapy. Physical therapy focuses on regaining mobility, muscle strengthening, gait training and improving range-of-motion of extremities. Occupational therapy addresses "activities of daily living." These are activities such as cleaning your teeth, setting a table - the things so many of us take for granted every day. They also address safety issues like locking a wheelchair before you stand up or how to walk with a walker. Many of our elderly forget that they are unable to walk, toilet themselves and many other everyday tasks. Judgment and cognitive skills are encouraged during therapy. Speech therapy and audiological services are also offered. Language skills and speech training, swallowing techniques and hearing issues are addressed on an individual basis.

Therapeutic recreation is a service often not recognized, but integral to the care and treatment of residents. Individual and group activities are designed to meet the needs of the residents. A wide variety of activities are offered to accommodate varying levels of care. Residents have opportunities to attend activities such as bingo, word games, ball toss, bowling, entertainment and many more programs which encourage cognitive and coordination skills. These are offered in a more relaxed and fun atmosphere.

Restorative nursing is a program that continues to help residents to maintain their full potential after formal therapy is finished. This is a program designed by the interdisciplinary team which focuses on needs of the resident. It may include exercise, ambulation, continence retraining and self-help. The nursing staff is made aware of the specific needs of the resident and time frames for these activities are set.

All nursing homes have wound care teams. These are interdisciplinary teams. Nurses assess residents weekly to monitor for skin conditions, and nursing assistants monitor residents' skin every time they give care. Any abnormalities seen are reported to the nurse who will immediately assess the resident and provide treatment as needed. A nurse who specializes in wound care will monitor the treatment's effectiveness and make recommendations. The medical doctor is called and recommendations are presented for approval.

Residents may enter a facility with wounds from surgery or from other causes. When wounds do not heal, visits to a wound care center may be required. These centers provide therapies that are not available in nursing homes. Recommendations are sent back with the resident when they return from the visit for continuing care. The wound care doctor and nursing home staff will work as a team until the wound is healed.

Individual Supervision

If you feel your loved one may need one-on-one attention this is the time to ask about it. What are the company policies? Some nursing homes assign nursing assistants to spend the shift on a one-on-one basis; others split the assignment among the staff on the floor. In these nursing homes you may see residents with nurses as they give meds, or walking with nursing assistants in hourly shifts. Constant supervision of a resident is not the same as having one-on-one attention from a staff member. Constant supervision means every staff member is asked to be aware of the resident and at times to stay with them, but no one is specifically assigned the task of watching the resident.

Residents who try to leave the facility unattended, or actually attempt to climb over a fence or break a lock to get out of the facility, may have Wanderguards placed on their wrists or ankles. These patients are candidates for one-on-one supervision. Others who need this kind of care may be those who express suicidal ideation or aggressive behavior toward another resident. Residents who have bad falls are also candidates for one-on-one supervision.

If you want to hire a private aide or companion to be with your loved one, question the policies at the facility. Due to government and insurance regulations, your private aide may be restricted to acting as a companion, doing errands or simply spending time talking, providing emotional support and comfort care. As your employee, a companion can report to you the general condition and other details of daily life in the facility. The facility social worker can help you find a companion if you wish. Be careful to check references before hiring and be specific regarding your expectations.

Some families hire companions to stay with loved ones for their whole stay in the facility; others have them stay during an adjustment period, and others do not feel they are necessary at all. Companion services should be tailored to the needs of your loved one.

Hospice Care

Nurses who work in a hospice-specific setting may be more comfortable giving end-of-life pain medications than a nurse who works in some other setting. Every nursing home I have worked in has offered hospice care or palliative care when a resident's condition has come to the point where comfort in dying is the main concern of family and medical staff. However, there are choices about hospice locations. Although many hospice patients are in nursing homes, there are also freestanding hospices in the community as well as hospitals. Hospice care can also be provided at home when the support is available.

If you are looking for hospice or palliative care, be sure to ask about regulations concerning overnight stays by family members should you or any member of your family want to be with a resident when they are nearing the end of life.

It would be beneficial to ask if family members can stay overnight with the hospice resident. There are times when families want to be close and give extra support, and it is good to know of any restrictions on visiting hours. Some facilities I have worked in have strict visiting hours where doors are locked at specific times and are reopened in the morning. If this is the case, ask if a call could be made to allow entrance into the building if you want to spend time with your loved one at the very end of life.

I personally have had very good experiences with hospice. My father-in-law died at home on hospice. The hospice service that cared for Dad was very involved, and provided nurses and support in caring for him. The nurses were wonderful during Dad's illness, and the follow up for my mother-in-law was very appreciated by her and all of us. My sister was also in hospice in a nursing home. My family is smaller than my husband's family and we were unable to provide the family support she needed to stay home. For those of us who lived out of the state, it was the best decision for her and her nearby family.

Chapter 2: Choosing the Nursing Home

Family Discussions

It is a good idea to sit down with your family and discuss your feelings about the decision you may have to make about nursing home placement. Be sure your loved one who is looking at the possibility of living in a nursing home is included in this discussion. The reality is that few people return to their homes once placed in long term care. This is the place where they will spend the rest of their lives and so it is important to include them in this conversation if possible.

Take a Tour

As an employee of a nursing home, I have often given tours to families and I always want to make the most favorable impression possible. I will show all aspects of the facility, but may avoid "problem" areas in which patients with dementia may act out, or parts of the building that may not be as presentable as others. You may want to come back several times and really look at the building, staff and other residents before making this important decision.

Have a list with you. Ask questions. Remember that the only "dumb" question is the one you didn't ask! If you thought the question, you need an answer. Time your visits: come during mealtime or ask if there are activities and when they are. Make it a point to see what happens at that activity. Look for interactions between staff and residents. Does the home have areas which appear to be convenient for staff to interact socially with the residents? Some nursing homes have tables set up near the nurse's station where residents can sit and have snacks, and where staff may be able to interact with them in a social and meaningful way.

Does the building look well-funded? Is it in good repair? As you walk around notice the structure and environment. Is it clean? Would you want to stay in that environment? Are the hallways unobstructed? Are they wide enough for wheelchairs to pass? What about the shower rooms? Are they stained or well maintained? Are there odors in the building? Know you can always return for another tour and address anything you may have overlooked.

Having space for wheelchairs to pass easily in hallways is very important for residents who have advanced dementia. They can become frustrated easily and may act out inappropriately when confronted with another resident who is in their way. It is also an advantage to have floors where the residents can walk in a square or circle without coming to a dead end. I have seen residents with advanced dementia become frustrated when facing a wall and act out in their distress.

As you walk through the nursing home it is always important to look at staff closely. How do they look? Are they interacting with the residents? Do they look relaxed? Are they smiling or do they look stressed and rushed? Ask what the ratio of staff to residents is.

How many residents are on a floor and how many nurses work each shift? In most facilities, day shift and the evening shift have two nurses giving medications and one on the desk. Night shift often has one nurse on a floor and a supervisor in the building. This supervisor covers the whole building.

Notice bells ringing; ask about the system the facility uses to answer call bells. Some facilities have in-house phone systems and when a bell is rung the aide receives a phone call and can easily answer just as you would your cell phone. This allows the nursing assistant or nurse to find out what the resident needs and respond appropriately.

In other homes, bells trigger a light over a resident's door while ringing at the nurse's station. When nurses see a light over residents' doors, there is no way to know which bell rang first. Bells are answered when seen, but not necessarily in the order in which they were rung. Be aware that aides have many residents to care for and may be caring for other residents when bells are rung. They cannot leave a resident who is at risk for falling alone in a bathroom or shower room to answer a bell. Staff may work as teams and answer each other's bells, but these staff members are more focused on their assigned residents than the other residents on the floor.

Chapter 3: Questions to ask

Food

Plan to visit the Dietary Department. What you eat has a great impact on your health, yet this is an area I have never been questioned about in all the tours I have given. You may want to sample the food and ask for a weekly menu to see if the choices will be accepted by your loved one. Remember that the diet is set to serve many dietary needs and you may find it bland.

Ask about special diets. What is their cardiac diet? What diet do they offer diabetics? You may even ask if you can come for a meal. Be sure if you do this that you do not specify when you will come so you are sure you are eating what the residents eat.

Ask: If my relative does not want to eat what is being served is there a substitute? Are snacks available at night? What are they?

Pets

Many facilities have pet regulations and because pets are so important in the lives of the elderly this is the time to ask about them. Usually a record of veterinary care is required for a pet visit. Are the shots up to date? Is the dog well mannered? Will the cat be brought in a carrier? Ask what regulations the facility has regarding pet visits.

Another issue to address with family members is what will happen to pets when their owners are no longer able to care for them. I have seen residents who mourned the loss of their pets long after coming to live in a nursing home. Many people consider pets to be part of their family and not knowing what has happened to a beloved pet can be a heart-wrenching issue. This issue is often not addressed in family discussions, but it can cause immense suffering to the family member who loves and feels responsible for their pets but can no longer provide for them. It's a good idea to know who will take over this responsibility. Just knowing that a pet is cared for and not dropped at the local shelter can make acceptance of placement in a nursing home much easier for the new resident.

I watch the faces of residents when family members bring their pets in to visit. It is amazing to see someone who is depressed or closed off talking to his or her pets. Even those who have become emotionally distant may 'wake up" and interact with life again, if only during that visit.

As an example, I recently had a resident who could not settle into the routine of the nursing home. She often seemed very upset, and as I was talking to her I learned she had a small, blind dog for 10 years. The dog was re-homed with a family friend and they had not bonded. I spoke to her and told her my family was looking for a rescue dog and would love to have her if she wanted to try another home. We now have the dog, which fits well with my family and frequently visits the nursing home to see her. I have seen such a change in my resident. She is more relaxed and happy.

Activities

If your family member likes to be active, ask what activities are available. Are residents mixed together in activities regardless of ability? Are there some activities for higher functioning residents? What are they? How many people attend?

In many facilities most activities serve the resident population with advanced dementia, who often form a large percentage of the population. You may want to ask if there are many people who will be able to interact with your family member on a cognitive level.

Are there bus tours for the residents? Do entertainers come in to present programs? How often? Where are the programs held? You may want to observe some activities you feel your loved one may be interested in attending.

Are there activities outside of the home?

Is there a van for resident use?

How often are out-of-facility trips planned for recreation?

Will the family be informed so they can arrange payment, and how?

Doctor visits

A big concern of my mother's is whether the doctor who cares for her in the facility will be the same one she had in the greater community. Ask any facility you are considering which doctors treat residents in the facility. Ask for information on the availability of the doctors to the residents and how often they visit their patients. Will they personally see my loved one? How often?

Ask:

Does our doctor have privileges in this facility?

What hospital do you use? How far away is it?

How often does the doctor see patients?

Will I have access to the doctor to ask questions?

Will you always inform me of changes in conditions?

Medical appointments?

Trips to the ER?

Room transfers?

Change of medication?

Results of tests and consults?

Who can I address my concerns to? Can you give me a business card with their contact information?

Is there an in-house pharmacy?

A medical suite for consultations?

Do you have nurse practitioners working in the facility? What hours are they available?

You may also want to discuss the availability of dentists, podiatrists and other doctors who may visit the facility and give resident care.

Finances

Finances are always a concern when considering placement in a nursing home. There are homes across the country which service a wide variety of people in diverse social circumstances. As laws are changing regarding elder care, it is best to ask a facility what their daily charge is for care. Ask:

What does this daily rate cover?

Are there additional charges?

How do we pay for this?

How much money can be retained when our loved one has "spent down" their money?

Is there someone on staff to help us apply for other monies available?

The Department of Public Welfare can be a wonderful resource for families making these difficult decisions. An elder attorney can be a great help. If you choose an attorney be sure to get references.

Laws are in effect at this time regarding transfer of property from those needing care to the caretaker. This property must be transferred at least five years prior to nursing home placement. There will be an investigation to determine that resources for payment of nursing home fees are reported and that no information is withheld. If it is found that resources are withheld in an attempt to hide assets, legal action may follow because this is an event which is "reportable" to governmental agencies.

Ask in what way these financial decisions will affect a spouse who remains at home. There are some funds that are not shared by spouses. These funds must be paid to the facility as payment for services (such as a 401K or other monies). When all the facility fees are paid any money left will go to the spouse when your loved one no longer needs their services. Be clear and specific with your questions so there are no financial surprises.

Payment schedules and services will be covered by the administration. Be sure to ask what is covered by insurance or other funds as well as what will come out of personal assets. If Social Security is to be transferred to the nursing home, will your loved one receive spending money? And if so, how much and when will they receive their money each month?

Visiting

Ask:

What about visits by friends and family? If you want to limit visiting by certain people ask how this can be done. The Power of Attorney can make it clear when they do not want certain family members or others visiting their loved one.

Are visiting hours at set times?

Where shall we park? Some older facilities have little parking facilities. Most staff members drive to work and may fill the parking lot. I find that the 7:00 to 3:00 staff is much larger than the 3:00 to 11:00 staff and parking is often better after 3:00pm.

What other regulations exist about visitors?

Are there ever times when visiting is not allowed? Under what circumstances would that happen? Has it happened in this facility?

Last year when the flu season was upon us and many of our residents and staff came down with the flu even though they had been given the flu shot, we were closed to visitors until the building was clear of the infection. This was for the safety of our frail and elderly residents. Some family members were very upset, while other appreciated the fact that we were trying to protect our population from further infection.

Chapter 4:   Making the Move

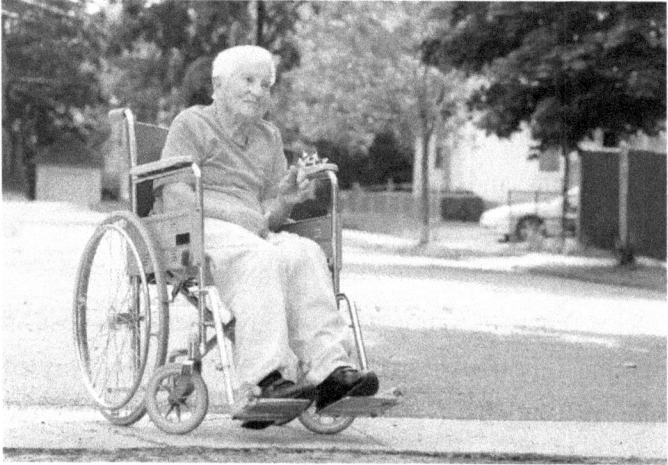

Once you have chosen the home you feel is best for your loved one you will want to talk to someone in the facility about admission. There are many issues you will cover. In all of this remember that your family member is the central figure and the goal is to provide the best care and support possible.

You may not be satisfied with your first choice of a residence. Although I find most people remain in a nursing home once they are admitted, it is possible to move to another facility if you desire. The social worker will help with this move (see Chapter 6 for more on the social worker's role).

Once you have made a decision, take the time to introduce your loved one to the facility. Take them on a tour if they haven't already been there. You may want to discuss what is important for them to take with them and how they want their new home to be prepared. Go over their possessions and decide what they want with them in their new home. Be aware that it is very difficult to give up almost all of your possessions and move into such a small space. Be prepared for emotional times as you prepare to transition into this immense life style change.

There is going to be a great sense of loss in making this transition. It is an entirely new way of life, and much of the independence enjoyed in the greater community is lost when an elder prepares to move into their new home. Change can confuse the elderly and increase their anxiety. Many families find this is a time when their care and support are needed the most by their relative.

The Room

If you have chosen a nursing home for your loved one you may want to consider a private room. I have met families who prefer their loved one live as well possible for as long as they can. Some of these families also hire private aides to provide comfort care and emotional support. When the money is gone the home will move your loved one into another room and apply for a government payment plan such as Medicaid.

Ask:

Can we decorate the room? Hang pictures?

Do you provide a TV and telephone in the room?

If not, where are the phones my relative can use? And who will be responsible to assist them to the phone?

Are husbands and wives able to share a room? If not, will they be on the same floor?

Also ask to see the specific room in which your loved one will be living. Ask about the temperature control in the room. Some residents require heat and others cold, and when people share a room who have different temperature requirements there are always problems. Usually the resident near the heater will have control of the temperature in the room simply because they may be able to turn the heat or air conditioner up or down whenever they feel uncomfortable.

Clothing

When you are packing your loved one's clothes, you need to consider the time of year it is and pack accordingly. Some people require warm clothes year round. For these people it is best to layer their clothing. There are also people who tend to be hot most of the time; they should also layer their clothes.

Storage space may be limited. Find out how big a closet you will be using. How many drawers are available to store clothing?

Most of my female residents wear slacks. Elastic waist slacks are best. They allow room for expansion as loved ones gain weight, which often happens as they become less active or are confined to a wheelchair. Some therapy departments suggest wearing sweat suits, which are comfortable and stretch with movement.

If it is possible you may want to color coordinate outfits using a color theme in all the clothes. Creating a "mix and match" wardrobe ensures that all outfits will look good. This can enhance your loved one's confidence and self-esteem – we always feel better when we feel we look good.

Shoes are also a concern. As we age, our balance and muscle tone can decline and the risk of falling is much greater. Sneakers have non-skid soles and give good support when walking.

If you take your loved one out to buy new shoes, be sure to buy extra socks. The socks should not be too tight. There are socks intended for diabetic patients which are comfortable and wick any moisture away from the feet. These socks are also more comfortable for anyone who has fluid retention in their feet. Be sure to buy enough pairs to allow your loved one to wear socks at night. We all lose heat through our feet and head and for those who tend to be cold, warm feet can help to ensure a good night's sleep.

Ask the facility if they provide locks for the closet and drawers. Request a spare key or ask if spare keys are kept in the facility should your loved one lose their key. Valuables such as checkbooks, credit cards and cash (except for a few dollars) should not be left in the room. Facilities have safes where these things can be kept, but it is best to take them home. Most facilities have "banks" where money can be safely held. You may want to ask what the banking hours are.

Jewelry can also be a concern. Some families replace expensive rings and necklaces with a less expensive piece that resembles the original piece. Residents may hide things from others and then forget where they put them and accuse someone of stealing. Many families have reported missing items only to find them wrapped in some article of clothing, or in a pocket. A resident may also lose weight and rings may no longer fit well and slide off of a finger. Another resident who is confused may wander into a room and take an item thinking it belongs to them.

Visitation

You may want to ask about Leave of Absence policies. What are the regulations regarding a visit home?

Some new residents enjoy going home for visits and continuing their family life as often as possible. They enjoy dinners at the homes of their children and interacting with grandchildren. Others may become anxious. I have seen residents refuse to go out the door for visits home once they have adjusted to the facility and feel safe living there. Some need to stay in the facility until they have better adjusted to avoid the unhappiness of returning to the building after a visit home. It is individual for each resident.

You also have the option of requesting the use of a room at the facility for special occasions such as a luncheon or birthday celebration. You may want to decorate it for the occasion and have it set up by staff. Most facilities provide a room without cost, but it is best to check first. You may also have to reserve the room if it is a holiday because many families may be celebrating at the same time.

You may want visit the facility often to discuss any concerns your loved one has as they adjust. Social services can provide a wonderful resource to support your loved one and their family.

Although most staff members try to meet the needs of those they care for, they cannot take the place of the familiar and loved ones at home, therefore your family member will need your love and understanding.

When you are planning to visit your loved one, it is considerate to not give the resident a specific time and date, unless you have made firm plans. I have seen residents sit at the front door of a nursing home from the time they get up in the morning until late at night waiting for a family member who said "I may come to visit you tomorrow." They often cry and are very upset and angry when they feel that no one is coming. If you come late you may be greeted with an angry, "Where have you been?" What you planned as a pleasant visit can become a nightmare quickly when emotions are high.

Visits from family make a great difference in the lives of residents in nursing homes. So many of our elderly and frail in the nursing homes get few or no visitors. They often appear to be forgotten. For these people, staff becomes their new "family." Those of us who work in long-term care for any length of time do it because we really like the elderly. We are the ones who encourage them to eat, spend time talking to them, and often hold their hands and stay with them in their last moments of life.

Our elders love to see their grandchildren and get great joy out of seeing them. However, when I take children to visit a resident, I never allowed them to crawl on the floor, and if a child is learning to walk and prone to falling I hold their hand or sit them down on a chair for the visit. I know that nursing homes are constantly cleaned, but I feel more comfortable knowing that I am protecting children from any possibility of picking up an infection.

If you are visiting in the room of your elder and it is nighttime, please be aware that a roommate may not be comfortable with someone visiting while they are in bed or using the bathroom. For times like this the facility will have an alternative, comfortable place for you to visit.

I have seen some families "adopt" roommates who become the friends of their loved one, who may have no family of their own to visit them. The generosity and kindness of such relationships always amazes me and the "adopted" resident has a richness added to their lives. It is always nice to remember that little things mean so much to them.

A roommate you have "adopted" may want to share something with you on a holiday to express their appreciation for you. I have seen residents get great joy out of giving a little something back to those who are kind to them. I once had a resident share a piece of candy with me that I knew was very, very old, but something she had saved because it was a touch point to remember someone cared enough to give it to her. I never eat such gifts, but I would never insult or hurt anyone by turning their generosity down. This is a gift from the heart of someone who has very little and wanted to share something which is special to him or her with me. It is always precious to me.

Many families enjoy taking Mom or Dad home for special occasions. It is best if you plan your visit carefully. If there is dementia, make it clear to the resident that they will come back to the nursing home. This prepares them for the return to the nursing home, and makes it easier for them when they return to the facility.

Consider what you will need for the visit. Are you able to get Mom or Dad in and out of the car and into your home? Will you need help with toileting? Do you have the supplies or equipment you may need? Can special transport be arranged when a resident is coming home for a visit? Or can nursing assistants be sent home to care for your loved one on the visit? What are the costs of transportation and a personal care aid? Who would make the arrangements?

Vans can be hired to transport your loved one and with attendants to assist them to get into the house. You may be able to hire an aide to come and help with personal needs. If you plan to provide transportation yourself and assistance is needed walking or going up steps you can ask the therapy department to teach you how to best help. Physical therapy can teach family members how to transfer, feed and toilet your loved one in a safe manner.

I would suggest you to speak to younger family members and encourage them to visit the nursing home. Talking, playing a simple game or pushing their wheelchair around the facility is the highlight of the residents' day, and gives them something to talk about with the other residents for quite some time after you leave.

I sometimes wonder why there are not more volunteers. The joy and pleasure volunteers bring to our residents simply cannot be easily explained. There are so many simple things that volunteers can do. Write a card and send it, come in to visit, bring a pet for a visit.

I have a friend with young children. In October she brings them in to visit dressed for Halloween in their costumes. The children hand out candy to many of our residents. Everyone has a great time; the children love it and so do the residents. It is the highlight of October!

I have another friend who went to a nursing home she visits to ask if they could have a "hat" day. She invited the ladies for tea and asked them to wear hats. She and I made our own hats and wore them. We took cheap swim caps and glued old artificial flowers on them making the worst looking hats we could. On the day of our tea we put our hats on our heads and collected our ladies. As we entered their rooms we would ask what they thought of our hats. The reactions we got made it was a fun day for all of us. We took pictures and presented them the next time we visited the home.

Another time I made a couple of pies and took them in for a small dessert after a short talk about healthy food. Be creative and have fun. There are all kinds of opportunities for volunteer work if we look for them.

Issues That May Arise

As a supervisor I have had the opportunity to hear many resident, family and staff complaints. I hope the following illustrations will help you understand life in nursing homes for both the resident and staff members.

Behavioral Issues

I have worked in nursing homes for over 20 years and I have found most people are good and kind. That being said, I feel that any population can be divided in many ways demographically. There will always be exceptional people and also those who are not good at all, but the majority of the people fall somewhere in the middle of the two extremes.

Several years ago I worked in a very exclusive nursing home where residents often wore very expensive jewelry. I had one resident who would put out inexpensive jewelry to see if the staff would steal it. She left rings and other jewelry on her dresser and watched to see if any of her aides would take the items. When I asked her why she did this stated she was curious and nothing was worth more than $500 anyway.

Another resident family complained bitterly that "Mother's" jewelry was missing. Her family felt staff should be fired and went to the Board Members to put pressure on the facility to find the "thieves" and remove them from the building. After "Mother" passed away I ran into her daughter in a local restaurant. I asked if they had ever found any of the jewelry. The daughter said yes, she had found it when she was going through her mother's clothes. It was wrapped in socks and other small articles of clothing. I asked if she had ever reported the finding to the nursing home. She replied, "No, I have the jewelry now and it doesn't make a difference." I responded that the facility would have appreciated knowing that the missing items were found and not taken.

On another occasion, I came into work and found the place in turmoil because a resident was missing a cell phone. The building was carefully searched by many of us and the phone couldn't be found. That evening after I had conducted yet another search, I called the woman's daughter and gave her a report of where I had looked and who I had spoken to looking for the phone. I asked her if she had taken anything home with her and she stated she had taken her Mother's laundry, but she knew it couldn't be in there. I asked her to check and there she found the phone. She was relieved, but did not express any regret for the way she shouted at our staff, or for the way she accused our aides and nurses of stealing.

In all the years I have worked in nursing homes only one man apologized for finding an item he thought was taken. I think it is human nature to speak out when we feel we are wronged, but it can be damaging to not apologize for poor judgment that reflected on others.

Residents will sometimes complain that other residents with dementia wander into their rooms and go thru their closets and dressers, on occasion taking things. Sometimes the confused patient will throw things on the floor or demand that the resident in the room leave their home or they will call the police. Other residents with dementia may climb into the bed and take a nap. These are always difficult situations. To address this problem we often put up "stop" signs, which hang across the door entrance. This will often stop residents with advanced dementia, but the signs must be taken down and put back each time the room's resident goes thru the door.

The nursing home I presently work in accepts many residents with diagnoses of Schizophrenia and Bipolar disease as well as advanced dementia. These residents can be very difficult to care for on a daily basis. They may refuse care, kick, bite, spit, scream, scratch and do any number of things to the staff giving direct care on a daily basis. I have a resident currently who curses and calls my aides names every day. Some aides tell me they cannot tolerate such disrespect and they often resign. There are others who tell me they knew the resident in better days, and know that she would be so embarrassed to know that she acts this way now.

The care and forgiveness I see for residents on a daily basis has affected me deeply. I give a lot of credit to my aides who deal with these behaviors. I am thankful for the staff that stays out of love of the elderly.

Residence management will often investigate after incidents like those just mentioned, to verify that the behaviors were not provoked. Policies are put in place to determine if there is a possibility of abuse of a resident. If abuse is suspected, the staff member in question must immediately leave the building and not return until a thorough investigation has been made. Abuse is not tolerated, and if proven, results in immediate termination.

Meals

There are often complaints about the food served in these facilities. Residents often do not like the food because it is not seasoned as they would season food at home. Because of the many diets that must be considered by the dietary department the food is often bland. There should always be a choice of meals available at the facility. Often a second meal is offered, or a sandwich. Some residents have the money and ability to call out and have food delivered.

Your loved one will be evaluated for their ability to swallow. If it is safer for your family member, diets may be downgraded to mechanical soft or ground foods. If your loved one will not eat food of this texture and you want to discuss the issue with the medical staff about changing the diet to one which is more to your loved one's liking, you will be asked to sign release forms stating that you know there is a possibility of aspiration. This form will state the risks that are inherent in this diet change and releases the facility from responsibility if the resident chokes or aspirates on their food. If you feel quality of life is important and it is in the best interest of your loved one, you can insist that they be allowed to eat a regular diet.

Residents on Hospice often return to a diet they prefer as a quality of life issue.

Eating is one of life's last pleasures and the elderly really enjoy sweets. If you want to surprise your loved one, cookies, ice cream and cakes are always great treats. And, water ice seems to be a favorite in the summer. The simple pleasure of a simple treat with loved ones can be the high point of someone's week.

A Change of Plans

If you are very unhappy with the facility you and your loved one chose, it is never a good idea to remove them against medical advice (AMA). If the patient is assessed and it is determined that it would be safe to go home, the facility's social worker will assist you in setting up any additional help or equipment you will need to care for them at home.

However, if you do not wait for these services to be put in place and take your loved one home without waiting for the doctor's assessment, or for proper help to be put in place, you will be asked to sign a form stating that the facility is no longer responsible for your loved one. Medications will not be sent home with you. Staff cannot help you with the move for legal reasons. The facility will be required by law to call the appropriate governmental agency and report that a resident was taken from the facility against medical advice.

<u>Chapter 5: End of Life Care</u>

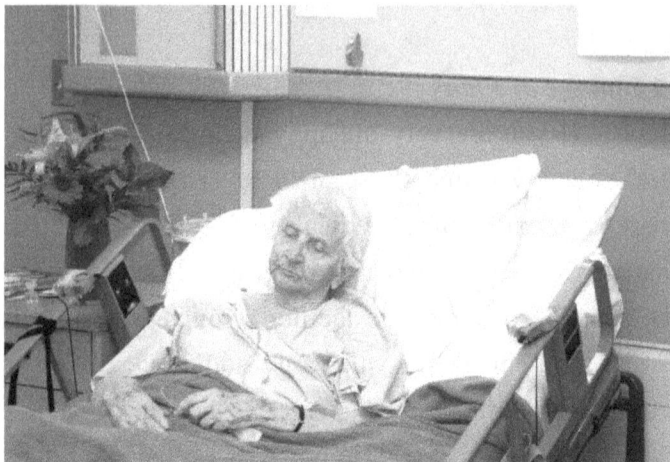

I find that many families have a difficult time when they must consider putting a loved one on comfort care or hospice. They may not be ready to let go or fear the emotional impact on their family when these services are initiated. The knowledge that these are end of life services and are based on comfort care and not prolonging life can be very difficult to face.

If this decision is made, expanded care promotes emotional health and wellbeing. If you choose hospice, more members are added to the team of caregivers for your loved one. Social workers and ministers can be very valuable in giving supportive care. Hospice care can include visits from family pets or a visit home, or other activities appropriate to the patient's condition. I have seen patients bundled up and taken outside in a snowstorm to see their last snowball fight. Another resident went on a picnic with family. This is a time to consider bringing a sense of completion to your loved one.

When the time comes to consider end-of-life options, your doctor will discuss all the choices with you, and if appropriate, your loved one. There are times when a doctor will feel it is too early to consider these services and will explain why he feels that way.

Sometimes the facility will contact the doctor and request he have a conversation with the Power of Attorney regarding your loved one's prognosis or wishes. Please keep an open mind and do only what is best for your loved one.

Some families feel guilty making these decisions. A living will can help you make a decision your loved one would be comfortable with, to allow you to move forward without guilt or family arguments. It is very important that the expressed desires of your elders be respected. If you do this you will know in your heart that you do not need to carry any guilt about the decisions you have made, for you have done your best.

Because eating is often one of our last pleasures, food and fluid restrictions may be lifted to allow residents to eat or drink things they really enjoy which were restricted due to medical conditions.

Medications may be discontinued when no longer appropriate or when your loved one can no longer swallow. Labs are also discontinued as well as appointments with specialists.

Once on hospice, it is the decision of the hospice team if a patient is to be sent to the hospital. However, the family does have the authority to overturn that decision. Hospice is a service that deals with end of life issues and it will be discontinued if your family chooses to prolong the life of your loved one. However, hospice will still be an option in the future if the family chooses it.

Sometimes our residents are sent to the hospital where they are told that Hospice is an option they should consider. Some hospitals offer hospice, but I find that families often prefer to have that their elderly members be with staff that they know and are comfortable with for the last moments of life. These are very personal decisions, but the welfare and desires of the person on hospice must be foremost in the mind of the family making these decisions.

Some patients do actually improve and come off hospice care for a time. Some may not show enough of a decline to stay on hospice, while others spend their last days on hospice. Each individual has his or her own path in life.

<u>Chapter 6: Getting Help</u>

The Social Worker's role

Social workers in nursing homes have many responsibilities. They are available to residents with complaints about the facility, staff or other residents. They also help to find money sources you may need to care for your loved one. If you are dissatisfied with the care or want to move your loved one to another facility, the social worker will make the necessary arrangements. She will also set up home care if your loved one is able to return home. She is a wonderful resource and can help you in many ways.

The social worker often facilitates a patient's care conferences, sometimes leading the discussion.

The conference is a time when all department heads and nursing staff come together with the Power of Attorney (POA) and any family or friends the POA invites to discuss your loved one's condition. This is a time to bring up your concerns and ask for resolution. It is often wise to bring a written list of topics you want to discuss. At the end of the conference, ask that someone be assigned to follow up on the things that were discussed in a timely manner and call you with the results.

Do not hesitate to call and request what you feel is needed for a more productive life for your family member. The worst response you could get is a polite "I'm sorry, I can't help with that." Remember, you won't know what can be done for you unless you ask.

Other resources

A great deal of information about nursing homes is available on the Internet. Google makes it easy to research a particular home. Remember that a business exists to make money. They will show you those things that are favorable to them on their website.

Information can come from many sources. Friends and family may be very helpful, sharing their experiences with nursing homes in the area in which you live. Your doctor may give recommendations and can tell you which facilities he is affiliated with if you want your loved one to remain under his care.

There are elder lawyers and governmental agencies such as the Department of Public Welfare and the Agency on Aging who can be very helpful. As the laws change often, it is best to use the resources available to get as much updated information as possible.

Nursing homes are inspected by government agencies. Their findings can also be found online. Be aware that this information can be confusing or misleading. For example, the nursing home I work in always gets a very high rating by the State inspectors and people misunderstand our "4" (usually out of possible "5" rating). They seem to think it refers to the physical facility, but it actually refers to the government survey of the care of residents. These families may be disappointed by the physical appearance of the facility when I take them for a tour. They cannot see that our nursing care is very good by looking at the building. In fact, some of our past volunteers have come to live with us because they know the quality of care we give. We also have a few retired nurses as patients who have worked in many facilities in this area and chose us over the "fancier" nursing homes.

Look beyond the number rating when reading a state inspection to see what the inspectors found in all departments. There is a lot of information given here, which applies to the daily running of the facility.

Chapter 7: You are doing the right thing!

Placement in a nursing home is a very difficult decision. There are so many things to take into consideration and discuss before the decision is made. It is best to start having conversations long before the possibility of placement presents itself. What is most important to the people you love? What are their preferences? Who will take over the care of pets? Will the spouse be living at home alone or with family? Review the questions in this book as you go through the process.

After a home has been chosen and you prepare your loved one for the transition, remember that it is difficult to give up all you have known and your freedom to choose when to eat, get up, shower, and so many other things. Know there will be a period of adjustment and a great sense of loss. It is difficult for any of us to downsize, but it is far more difficult to move into a small room that is shared with a stranger, leaving most of your belongings behind. Be patient and supportive during the process.

Be patient as your loved one accepts the fact that they may never go home to live again. This is very possibly their home for the rest of their life. As this realization comes to them they may be depressed or angry. This is a time to reassure them that you do love them and are doing what is best for everyone.

Your loved one is the center of all these decisions and will require patience, love and support throughout the transition and period of adjusting to a new living environment.

Conclusion

As a nurse who has worked in many nursing homes, the poem below really touches my heart. It was reportedly written by a woman who died in the geriatric ward of a Scottish hospital. It was found among her possessions and so impressed the staff that copies were made and distributed to every nurse in the hospital.

So many of the nurses I have worked with are very aware that today's nursing homes are businesses and as such are always looking at the "bottom-line" to make money. Due to time constraints the social needs of our residents often go unmet as we give our medications, do treatments and all the other little detail things that must be done to meet the medical needs of our residents.

The days are long gone when I had time to sit and learn about my residents. Who are they? Did they have children? What books do they like? Do they like to sit outside in warm weather? These are the little things that made their lives special and made them who they are. We need to recognize that theirs is the generation that saw the first airplanes, jets, computers, televisions and so many other "firsts". They have wonderful stories to tell and these stories should be a gift to those of us who follow them.

Even their families may see these wonderful elders in a new light, as the poem's author in the nursing home felt the staff saw her. My hope is that those who read this book will realize that our elderly need our support and love. Family is precious to them and even kind, considerate staff members cannot provide the emotional and social support they need and look for from family.

80

What Do You See, Nurse?

What do you see, nurse... what do you see?
Are you thinking - when you look at me:
"A crabbed old woman, not very wise;
Uncertain of habit with far-away eyes,
Who dribbles her food and makes no reply
When you say in a loud voice 'I do wish you'd try.'"
Who seems not to notice the things that you do
And forever is losing a stocking or shoe;
Who, resisting or not, lets you do as you will
With bathing and feeding, the long day to fill.
Is that what you're thinking, is that what you see?
Then open your eyes, nurse. You're not looking at me!
I'll tell you who I am as I sit here so still.
As I move at your bidding, eat at your will:
- I'm a small child of ten with a father and mother,
Brothers and sisters who love one another;
- A young girl of sixteen with wings on her feet,
Dreaming that soon a love she'll meet;
- A bride at twenty, my heart gives a leap,
Remembering the vows that I promised to keep;
- At twenty-five now I have young of my own
Who need me to build a secure, happy home.
- A woman of thirty, my young now grow fast.
Bound together with ties that should last.
- At forty, my young sons have grown up and gone,

But my man's beside me to see I don't mourn;
- At fifty once more babies play 'round my knee
Again we know children, my loved ones and me...
Dark days are upon me, my husband is dead.
I look at the future, I shudder with dread.
For my young are all rearing young of their own,
And I think of the years and the love that I've known.
I'm an old woman now, and nature is cruel.
'Tis her jest to make old age look like a fool.
The body, it crumbles, grace and vigor depart.
There is a stone where I once had a heart.
But inside this old carcass a young girl still dwells,
And now again my bittered heart swells;
I remember the joys, I remember the pain
and I'm loving and living life over again;
I think of the years, all too few, gone too fast
And accept the stark fact that nothing can last;
So open your eyes, nurse, open and see... not a
crabbed old woman.
Look closer... see me!

ॐ

NURSE'S RESPONSE - Author Unknown

What do we see, you ask, what do we see?
Yes, we are thinking when looking at thee!
We may seem to be hard when we hurry and fuss,
But there's many of you, and too few of us.
We would like far more time to sit by you and talk,
To bathe you and feed you and help you to walk.
To hear of your lives and the things you have done;
Your childhood, your husband, your daughter, and
your son.
But time is against us, there's too much to do –
Patients too many, and nurses too few.
We grieve when we see you so sad and alone,
With nobody near you, no friends of your own.
We feel all your pain, and know of your fear
That nobody cares now your end is so near.
But nurses are people with feelings as well,
And when we're together you'll often hear tell
Of the dearest old Gran in the very end bed,
And the lovely old Dad, and the things that he said,
We speak with compassion and love, and feel sad
When we think of your lives and the joy that you've
had.
When the time has arrived for you to depart,
You leave us behind with an ache in our heart.

When you sleep the long sleep, no more worry or care, There are other old people, and we must be there.

So please understand if we hurry and fuss –
There are many of you, and too few of us.

જી